ERIC GAGNÉ

BREAK BARRIERS

Positively For Kids®
811 Kirkland Avenue, Suite 200
Kirkland, WA 98033
www.positivelyforkids.com

Gagné, Eric, 1976-
Eric Gagné—break barriers/ by Eric Gagné with Greg Brown.
48p. :ill. (mostly col.), ports.; 26 cm (...series...)
Summary: Details the life of Eric Gagné, Cy Young Award® winning pitcher for the
Los Angeles Dodgers, and how positive thinking enables him to break all barriers.
Audience: Grades 4-8

ISBN 0-9634650-6-6

I. Gagné, Eric, 1976-. Juvenile literature. 2. Baseball players—United States—
Biography—Juvenile literature. [1. Eric, Gagné, 1976-. 2. Baseball players—
Biography.] I. Brown, Greg, 1957-. II. Title.

796.357/092—dc21[B]

Library of Congress Control Number:
2004I030708

Photo Credits:
All photos courtesy of Eric Gagné and family except the following:
Jim Thompson/Albuquerque Journal: 31. AP/Wide World: 35 bottom right;
37 bottom right; 40; 43 top right; 43 bottom right; 45. Dominic Campeau: 25 left;
25 bottom right. Tom Dipace: 6. Getty Images: 3; 29; 35 top right; 35 bottom left;
35 top right; 36; 37 bottom left; 44 left; 47. Los Angeles Dodgers: cover; 5 right;
35 top left; 35 middle left; 37 top left; 37 top middle; 37 top right; 37 bottom
middle; 38; 39; 43 left. Montreal Canadiens: 44 right. National Baseball Hall of
Fame: 41 left. Milo Stewart Jr./NBLA: 41 right. San Antonio Missions Baseball Club:
32 left; 32 right.

Special Thanks:
Positively For Kids would like to thank the people and organizations that helped
make this book possible: Eric and Valerie Gagné; the Gagné family; Peter Caparis
and Kristen Anderson of Impact Marketing Solutions; Martin Leclerc;
Lloyd Simmons; and the Los Angeles Dodgers.

Book Design:
Methodologie, Inc., Seattle

Printed in Canada

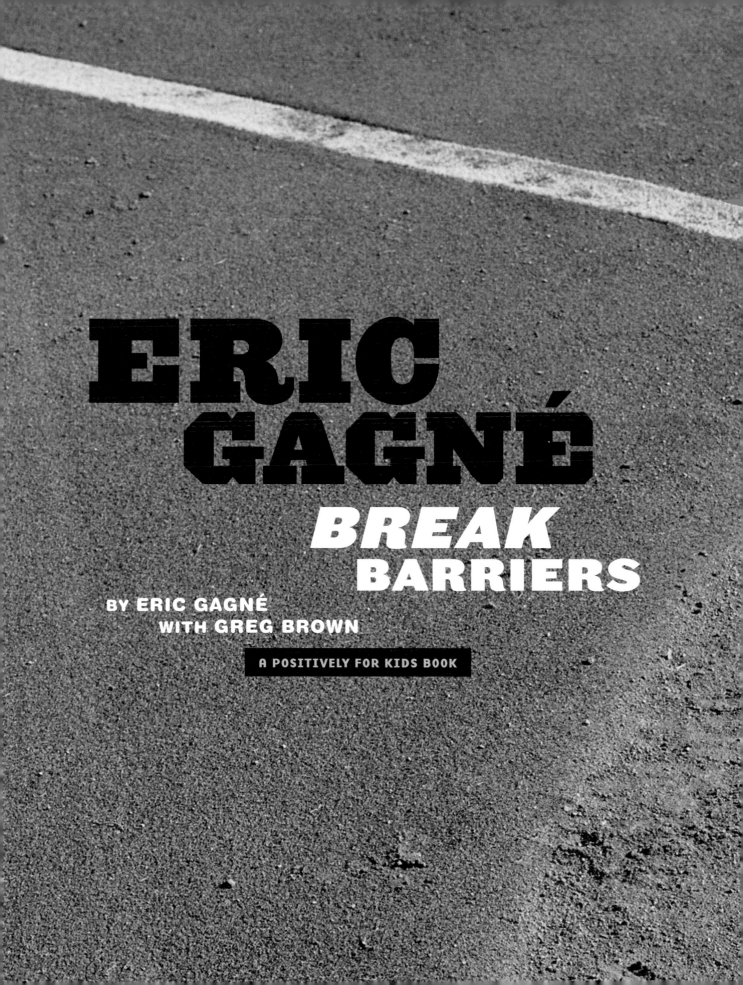

ERIC GAGNÉ

BREAK BARRIERS

BY ERIC GAGNÉ
WITH GREG BROWN

A POSITIVELY FOR KIDS BOOK

Hi. I'm Eric Gagné (pronounced GONE-yea).

If my last name sounds strange to you, that's because I'm from Montreal, Quebec, in Canada. Most people living there speak French.

Being a closer in baseball means it's my job to pitch in the last few innings to save the game. When I play, the game is on the line. That creates stress and nervousness.

To many, the pressure of performing in stressful situations is a barrier standing in the way of their success.

I know all about barriers, and I'm not talking about just the barriers I've faced in baseball.

I know the barrier of not having enough money. I know the family barrier created by divorce. I know the barrier of shyness. I know the barrier of living in the United States without knowing a word of English. I know the barrier of facing a career-ending injury. I know the barrier of being demoted and failing.

And I know about the biggest barriers of all—the barriers buried in our own minds. I know the pain of hiding an eating disorder.

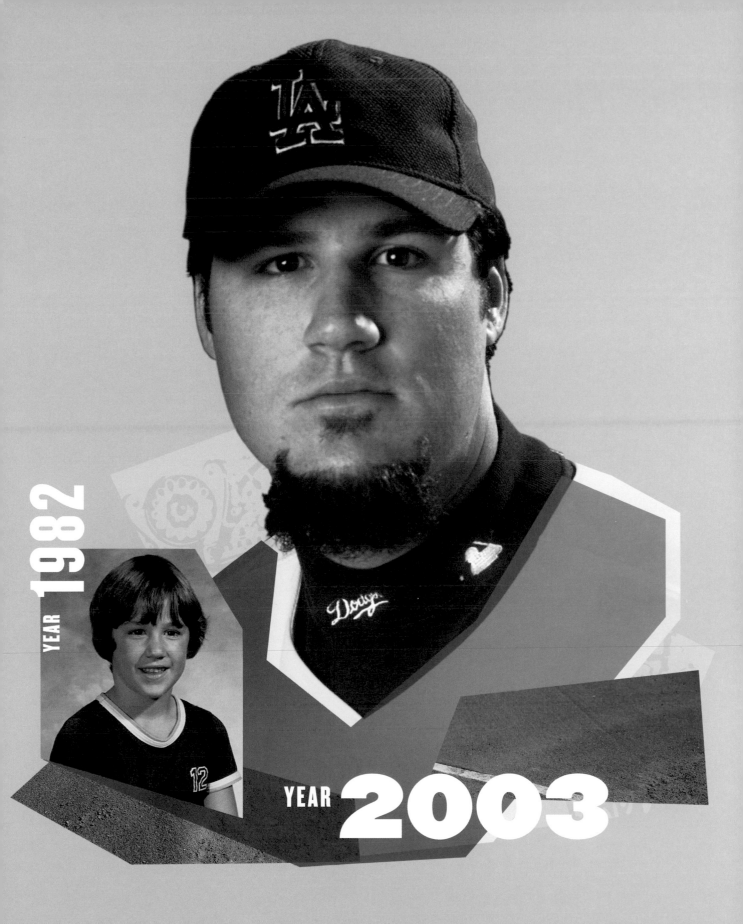

YEAR **1982**

YEAR **2003**

I also know about the pressure of performing with 50,000 fans screaming either with me or against me and the baseball game is in my hands. It's a thrilling, energizing, nerve-tingling, and scary feeling all in one.

When I enter a game at Dodger Stadium, the crowd goes crazy. The high-energy song "Welcome to the Jungle" blasts throughout. The scoreboard flashes "Game Over."

During the 2003 season I had a magical run, going 55-0 in save opportunities to set a Major League record. My perfect season earned me the Cy Young Award®, given to each league's top pitcher. It was only the second time a Canadian pitcher won the award.

Yes, the 2003 season was amazing, but not as amazing as everything that's happened in my life to put me in the position to break barriers.

I've written this book to share with you true stories about my life. My hope is that this book will help you break through barriers you face, real and imagined.

> The small pictures show me at play with my brother and dad teaching me horseshoes.

> This is the house where I grew up. I guess we liked yellow. I had a yellow bike and Dad had a yellow car.

I grew up in Mascouche (pronounced moss cooch), just outside of Montreal.

While most Canadians speak English, the settlers in Quebec were mostly from France. Generations have stubbornly held onto their French language. I grew up speaking only French. It's almost like Quebec is its own little country.

We lived in a modest three-bedroom house in a middle-class neighborhood. In Montreal it seems everyone is middle-class. More than 3 million people live in the Montreal area, yet it seems like one big hard-working family.

My father, Richard, worked as a bus driver for the city of Montreal. My mother, Carole, was a waitress. We never lacked anything we needed, but we didn't always have what we wanted.

I have one younger brother, Dominic. Raising two active boys probably drove my parents a little crazy. Dad was strict, but fair and loving. Mom was always there for us, a very good listener and always happy.

I had a great childhood full of sports. We watched hockey and baseball on TV as a family. I remember going to bed before the games were over and sneaking downstairs to watch the end. Dad saw me out of the corner of his eye and always let me stay.

I'D WATCH THE MONTREAL EXPOS ON TV AND WE ATTENDED SOME GAMES EVERY YEAR. WE COULDN'T AFFORD HOCKEY TICKETS. BASEBALL WAS A MAGNET. THE MORE I WATCHED, THE MORE I LIKED THE SPORT.

Mascouche, Quebec
MANITOBA
York Factory
Sleeper Is
Belcher Is
Ft Severn
Norway House
SEVERN
LAKE WINNIPEG
Ft Chimo
Schefferville
JAMES BAY
FT GEORGE
Ft George
Ft Albany
ALBANY
LAKE OF THE WOODS
Winnipeg
Thunder Bay
ONTARIO
QUEBEC
Goose Bay
Moosonee
L MISTASSINI
MINN
Duluth
L SUPERIOR
Cochrane
Superior
Sault Ste Marie
LAWRENCE
Quebec
Rimouski
GULF
ST
Charlottetown
PEI
Fredericton
NB
Halifax
NOVA SCOTIA
St. Paul
WIS
Green Bay
MICH
L HURON
Madison
Milwaukee
Montreal
MAINE
VT
Augusta
Montpelier
NH
Concord
Sable
Yarmouth
Toronto
L ONT
N Y
Chicago
Lansing
London
Detroit
Toledo
L ERIE
Windsor
Rochester
Buffalo
Albany
MASS
Boston
Hart
RI
CONN
Providence
ILL
Gary
Springfield
IND
OHIO
Cleveland
Columbus
PA
Pittsburgh
New York
Indianapolis
Cincinnati
Harrisburg
Trenton
NJ
St. Louis
Louisville
Baltimore
MD
Philadelphia
MO
OHIO
Charleston
W VA
KY
Frankfort
Dover
DEL
Washington
TENN
Nashville
Richmond
VA.
Memphis
APPALACHIAN MTS
Chattanooga
NC
C Hatteras
Birmingham
ALA
GA
Raleigh
MISS
SC
Atlanta
Montgomery
Columbia
Augusta
Charleston
Mobile
Columbus
Savannah
Tallahassee
New Orleans
Jacksonville
St Petersburg
FLA
Tampa
C. Canaveral
Ft
BAHAMAS
MEXICO
Bermuda
(Br.)

> My first goatee!

For most Canadian boys, there are a number of baseball barriers. First off, hockey is the No. I sport in Canada. There are more youth hockey teams and better organizations than baseball, which is seen as something to do between hockey seasons. Boys are encouraged to ice skate and play hockey at early ages. I was. And I played hockey like everyone else, and loved every minute. I will say baseball's popularity in Canada is growing.

THE OTHER OBSTACLE IS OUR SEASON IS SO SHORT. BEING SO FAR NORTH, BASEBALL HAS JUST A THREE-MONTH SEASON IN QUEBEC BECAUSE OF THE COLD, WET WEATHER.

My dad says I started throwing a baseball when I was 2. He says I had perfect natural form.

Dad and a friend sometimes played catch in our backyard with a softball. One day I was in the middle of their game of catch. They teased me by throwing it over my head as I tried to jump up and "steal" the ball.

On one throw, however, Dad misjudged my jump and he threw the ball right into my face. Dad thought he really hurt me. With tears in my eyes, I said, "Let's keep playing."

Dad could tell I loved baseball so he didn't let the lack of organized teams for young kids be a barrier to me. He started organizing pickup baseball games when I was 5. He'd drive around the neighborhood in his yellow Malibu and cram in about 10 kids and drive us to the neighborhood baseball field.

We'd play practice games. I'd be so excited to play, I'd wear an all-white uniform while everyone else was in jeans and T-shirts.

When I graduated to organized baseball at the age of 7, a funny thing happened at one of my first tee-ball games. A TV crew happened to be looking for young kids playing baseball. They found our game and videotaped our action. I hit a home run. After the game, a reporter interviewed me on TV. He asked what I wanted to be when I grew up.

"A Major League pitcher," I said confidently. That was a little strange because I didn't pitch. I played third base. I didn't start pitching until I was 14.

> I had an adventurous spirit growing up. From my first fishing trip, to playing in the forest, to drenching myself, to playing the harmonica, I wasn't afraid of trying new things.

It didn't matter what position I played during grade school. What upset me most was not playing.

Whenever our baseball games were rained out, I cried. Because of our short season, rainouts weren't rescheduled. If a game was rained out, I became very upset and made Dad at least play catch once the rain stopped.

Scary movies also upset me. I'd be brave and watch them, but when it came time to sleep, I'd have these terrible images in my head. I didn't want to be alone in my room. I had a special blanket, like most kids. I slept with that blanket until I was about 13 and it helped soothe my fears.

Some nights, however, I'd go into Dominic's room and sleep on the floor next to his bed. I did that off and on until I was 12.

A game I played with my childhood friend scared our parents a little. Dave Gaudreault and I played "Lost Child."

We built little branch cabins in the forest about a mile from our houses and pretended we were lost in the woods. Some days we'd be gone from 8 in the morning until 6 at night.

WE ALWAYS KNEW WHERE WE WERE. BESIDES AT DINNERTIME, USUALLY AROUND 6, DAD WHISTLED FOR ME TO COME HOME. I SWEAR WE COULD HEAR HIS PIERCING WHISTLE THREE MILES AWAY. HE WAS STRICT ABOUT ME MISSING DINNER SO I ALWAYS RAN HOME.

Dave and I became best friends. We were such good friends I'd split my lunch with him at school.

Several times a week Dave didn't have any money for lunch or didn't like the lunch he had. I always got $3 a day for lunch. We'd always get two hotdogs, one for each, and split a bag of french fries. Dave and I have stayed close friends over the years. We've helped each other in many ways. I've encouraged him when his carpenter business wasn't doing so well, and he's picked me up when I've been down.

FUN FACT >>> ERIC OFTEN WENT TO EXPOS GAMES EARLY TO ROAM THE BLEACHERS DURING BATTING PRACTICE. HE COLLECTED "A LOT" OF HOME-RUN BALLS.

15

> I spent most of my free time playing outside with friends. I did study some of the time and was proud to advance from each grade level.

As I got older, I never wanted to stay inside and play video games. I always wanted to be outside. We played neighborhood ice hockey in the winter and street hockey in warm weather. I was one of the older guys and always made sure the younger kids had a chance to play with us. I never wanted to put barriers around people and keep them out. I didn't want anyone to feel left out.

We didn't always have enough hockey pads for everyone. I always made sure my little brother had all the gear he needed, even if I played without pads. Sometimes I even played goalie with just a stick and glove.

We were good kids who liked to have fun. Once we did act a little naughty.

Instead of playing sports one day, we decided to ride our bikes around and knock over people's garbage cans. We were hoping someone would come out and chase us. We got our wish when a gruff old man, who frightened everyone, hopped in his car and came after us.

"I'M GOING TO CALL THE POLICE ON YOU BOYS!" HE YELLED. WE WERE SO AFRAID OF GOING TO JAIL, WE QUICKLY CHANGED CLOTHES SO WE WOULDN'T BE RECOGNIZED. WE WERE SO SCARED WE NEVER TIPPED OVER TRASH CANS AGAIN.

Picking up trash around our house, or any housework for that matter, is what I hated to do most.

With just us two boys making messes, my parents finally got fed up with it and made us a deal. They agreed to pay us to clean house.

Dominic and I wanted to have some change in our pockets, so we'd get $2 for vacuuming, $1 for making our beds and $1 for washing the dishes. We could make about $15–$20 a week and our house never looked cleaner.

Besides my job as a professional baseball player, I've had three other real jobs.

First, I decided to be a paper boy at age 11. My route delivering newspapers was long and brutal. I'd wake up at 4 every morning and worked 2 1/2 hours before breakfast and school. I lasted only four months.

When I was a teenager, Mom got me a job as an assistant cook at the restaurant where she worked. I lasted two years.

A winter after playing in the minor leagues, I worked 12-hour shifts as a security guard at a security firm. Funny thing about that was people recognized me as a baseball player from newspaper and TV reports and wondered why I was working. They thought I was making millions. I made about $850 a month in the minor leagues so I needed a winter job.

Going to midnight mass on Christmas Eve was a Gagné family tradition that almost seemed like a job.

Many families have that tradition. But ours included a twist. We had to walk to church and home, no matter the weather.

The 30-minute walk could have been a sled-dog race it seemed so far, usually in bitter cold weather with snow falling.

Dad got the worst of it when we were small. We'd fall asleep at church and he'd have to carry us home.

> My first two jobs were working as a newspaper boy and working in a restaurant kitchen.

FUN FACT >>> ERIC NEVER ASKED AN EXPOS PLAYER FOR AN AUTOGRAPH AS A CHILD. HE DIDN'T HAVE THE COURAGE, HE SAYS. HE DID GET BASEBALLS AUTOGRAPHED BY EXPOS AT BASEBALL CAMPS HE ATTENDED DURING HIS TEEN YEARS.

Twice Dad saw me "fall asleep" after blows to my head during sports competitions.

I suffered a concussion while Dad and I were playing racquetball. We were very competitive when we played each other in sports (and still are). He hit a short shot. I dove for it, and hit my head against the wall. I was out only a few minutes, but Dad feared the worst.

Another time, a dirty hockey play knocked me out when I was I5. Someone hit me in the back and slammed my head against the boards.

IT KNOCKED ME OUT COLD. I STAYED IN THE HOSPITAL ALMOST TWO DAYS BECAUSE I COULDN'T REMEMBER A THING, AND I KEPT THROWING UP. THANKFULLY, MY MEMORY RETURNED.

I put a friend's brother in the hospital once thanks to a freak slap shot.

It happened at a youth hockey tournament. We were staying in people's cabins. There wasn't a nearby rink, so creative thinking overcame that barrier. We thought it would be fun to hit slap shots against a door. A teammate's brother stood on the other side of the door. We warned him to close the door, but he didn't listen.

My first shot accidentally blasted through a 6-inch door opening and cracked the younger brother in the face. He needed about 20 stitches near his cheekbone, which you can still see today.

I can thank hockey for two other injuries. I hurt my knee during a game at age 17, but never needed surgery, fortunately. A high stick to an eye is the reason I wear those goggle eye glasses when I pitch. The eye injury didn't hurt my eyesight. It scarred my left eye, so I couldn't wear contacts when my vision faded.

> I loved every minute of playing hockey. Being on teams taught me how to get along with others and how to compete.

I SOMETIMES WONDER HOW FAR I COULD'VE GONE IN HOCKEY. I SKATED WELL, COULD DRIBBLE THE PUCK, AND HAD A GOOD SLAP SHOT. I TELL PEOPLE I PLAYED THE GOON ROLE, BUT ACTUALLY, I WAS A DECENT ALL-AROUND PLAYER. EVERYONE CALLED ME "THE TRAIN" BECAUSE NOBODY COULD STOP ME ON THE ICE.

I reached Midget 2AA in hockey. But the time commitment for both sports became too much. I had to pick one at age 17.

I started leaning towards baseball two years before. That's when I moved out of my parents' home at 15 to live with two other teenagers in an apartment.

Hockey 92-93

The only school in the area with a baseball program was in Montreal. Most schools in Quebec don't have baseball teams. Boys play mostly on summer teams with only about 20 games a year. I convinced my parents this was the right thing for me. It proved to be a big step.

Fortunately, I roomed with two great guys, both a couple years older, who took school seriously and kept me focused on what I needed to do. I really didn't want to study much in 10th through 12th grades. I was an average student. Not surprisingly, my favorite class became physical education.

French is the only class I failed, and not because I didn't know the language. I failed because of my shyness.

This one French teacher required students to give a presentation in front of the class. A few minutes into my 20-minute speech my mind went blank. I couldn't speak. My mind froze. I cracked under the pressure. It embarrassed me so much I refused to try it again.

The teacher ruled either I give my speech to the class or I'd fail. The pressure of speaking in front of people paralyzed me. My mind made the barrier so high, I refused to try. So I flunked.

I passed most summer tests on the baseball diamond. I started getting serious about pitching at 14. My regular position then was third base. I had a good glove, strong arm, hit with power, but couldn't run too fast.

I got my chance at pitcher because all our pitchers were injured in a tournament.

When I play baseball, I'm always serious about winning. I become intense. I have always loved feeling the pressure of the game. The pressure of winning always pumped me up. I never feared it.

From early on I always had a strong desire to win. When teammates made errors behind me, it angered me. I didn't say anything, but you could see the fire in my eyes. I remember one game when errors cost us four runs in the first couple innings. I took matters into my own hands and struck out everyone the rest of the way. We won 5-4.

I didn't know how hard I threw until baseball scouts with radar guns came to a game when I was 17.

I started and felt strong. People crowded around the scouts behind the backstop to see the radar readings. Word spread quickly.

BY THE TIME I REACHED THE DUGOUT AFTER THE FIRST INNING A YOUNG KID RAN UP TO ME ALL EXCITED: "ERIC, YOU'RE THROWING 90 MILES PER HOUR!"

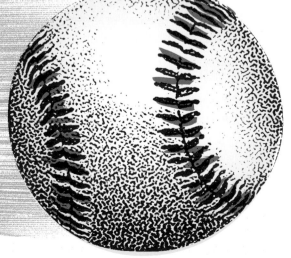

I thought maybe I was throwing 85. I had no idea. Hitting 90 is a magic number for pitching prospects and it put me on the scouting radar. Scouts started talking to me after games. My dad gave me some great advice then. He said not to get too excited or depressed by what anyone said to me. This would be just the beginning. He was right.

A SPORTSWRITER FROM MONTREAL, MARTIN LECLERC, STARTED FOLLOWING MY CAREER. HE WROTE ABOUT MY VICTORIES AND CALLED ME COCKY AND REBELLIOUS. I DIDN'T MIND THAT, IT WAS TRUE. I ADMIT I'M A FREE SPIRIT.

BASEBALL CANADA
National Selects Championship
Moncton, N.B.

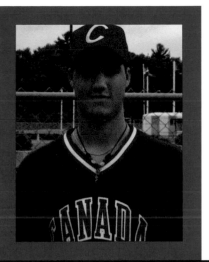

> The Canadian National Team and I laugh it up during a road trip.

> I really wasn't sleepwalking in the picture above—I guess I blinked at the wrong time.

He also wrote that I didn't work hard enough. I couldn't believe it. Yes, I was a little pudgy, and I didn't like the body I saw in the mirror, but that was my problem. How could he write that? I would understand later.

That summer I earned a spot on the Canadian National Team. I became friends with the only other French-speaking teammate, Dominic Campeau, our catcher. My highlight of the summer came when I shut down Team USA in the ninth inning. I came in with two runners on base with Canada holding a one-run lead. I retired Troy Glaus, struck out the next batter, and then ended the game with three straight strikes past J.D. Drew.

The next summer I had a perfect season. I didn't give up an earned run for the national team the whole season. Unfortunately, we just missed qualifying for the 1996 Olympics with a loss to Nicaragua.

The Chicago White Sox drafted me in the 30th round, which is very low. I had college scholarship offers. I decided to attend one of the top junior college baseball programs in the States. I enrolled at Seminole State College in Oklahoma.

I HAD A HUGE LANGUAGE BARRIER TO OVERCOME. I COULDN'T SPEAK ANY ENGLISH. I WATCHED HOURS OF MTV TO LEARN THE LANGUAGE. I GAVE MYSELF A CRASH COURSE IN ENGLISH JUST TO SURVIVE.

It was the toughest thing I've done, besides staying in Oklahoma. I became homesick after two weeks.

My parents had just divorced and my mother wasn't feeling well. I wanted to go home and help her.

I spoke to our coach, Lloyd Simmons, about it. He said human beings are meant to make adjustments. That's why we've been on earth so long. "Why don't you give it two more weeks and see what happens," he said.

The only word that came to mind was "whatever."

Two weeks later I still wanted to go home. When times get tough, negative thoughts flow in as naturally as water flows downhill.

"Coach, I'm not going to make it here," I insisted. "I need to go home."

"You start something, you finish it," Simmons said as if it was the law. It hit home because my dad drilled the same message in my head. Simmons challenged me.

"Fine, go home," he said. "But I won't buy you a ticket home."

I didn't have enough money to get home, so I stayed. If Mom truly needed me I would have hitchhiked home. But I was looking for an easy way out of my problems.

> My first few weeks at
Seminole State College in
Oklahoma I didn't smile
much. I wanted to go home.

Coach Simmons taught me a great lesson about how persistence does break down barriers. I stuck it out. I entered college with a soft body and stood about 5-foot-10. I left with a strong mind and body and grew several inches, too.

Coach Simmons, who set a record as the winningest college baseball coach at any level, is old school. He's tough, but fair. Best of all he set a great example. In 26 years as coach, his teams went to the Junior College World Series 13 times. None of his teams ever won it all. Still, he remained excited to coach baseball every day and was optimistic. Plus, he'd do all the 5 a.m. workouts we did.

I WAS ALWAYS COMPETITIVE, BUT COACH SIMMONS TAUGHT ME ABOUT BEING DISCIPLINED AND WORKING HARD.
HE SAID YOU HAVE TO WORK HARD TO BE GREAT AT ANYTHING—ANYBODY CAN BE AVERAGE.

Winning under pressure isn't always about winning a championship or being No. 1. Coach Simmons showed me it's about doing your best to prepare and then giving your best. Coach Simmons retired from college coaching and now coaches in the Kansas City Royals minor-league system.

I spent only one year at Seminole State College. Our team went to the Junior College World Series and finished third. I had a solid year, 11-0, with a 1.30 earned run average as a third starter. The Dodgers took notice, and I signed as a free agent after the season.

I began my professional career with forgettable failure—losing the first six games I started. Then I felt a pop in my elbow on a pitch and lost the feeling in my last two fingers. I sat out a month to rest my arm.

Just when I thought things couldn't get worse I confronted a secret I'd been hiding for two years.

After my parents divorced I struggled with an eating disorder—it wasn't overeating. I wasn't eating enough. I lost my appetite. That probably sounds strange for a guy 6-foot-2, 240 pounds, but it's true. I'd go through a day and eat only a cookie and drink a glass of milk. I didn't feel like eating.

I got through it for a year, but with the Dodgers I pushed my body working out every day. I started feeling dizzy on the mound and lost strength. My coaches noticed something was wrong.

Finally, I found the courage to talk about it with our trainers and a team psychologist. Talking about it made all the difference. It started bringing down those barriers in my head. I realized to continue in baseball, I had to give my body the fuel it needed to perform. Baseball became my motivation to eat.

When I came back, I pitched despite pain in my elbow and won nine straight starts to finish the season 9-6.

THE NEXT SEASON, AT SPRING TRAINING, I WOKE UP AND LOOKED AT MY ARM IN HORROR. IT HAD TURNED DODGER BLUE.

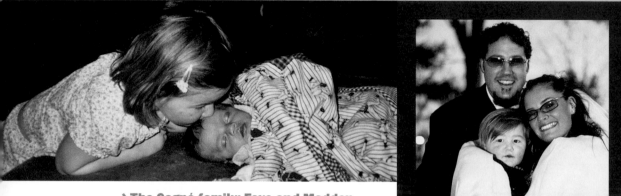

> The Gagné family: Faye and Maddox (above) and Valerie, Faye, and me.

Team doctors explained I tore ligaments in my elbow and needed surgery; 23 years earlier it would have ended my career. But Tommy John, a veteran pitcher, proved in 1974 that it's possible to come back from ligament elbow surgery. Now the procedure is named after him.

My surgery went well, but I couldn't lift a ball or pick up anything for six months during 1997. That drove me crazy. I'm not real patient. This was a tough time for me. The pressure of the unknown is hard to handle. I had up and down days. I had to think only about what I could do each day and not worry about the future.

Some barriers force you to go in a different direction. I considered accepting a hockey scholarship to the University of Vermont and retiring from baseball.

I went back home and lived with Mom. There I reconnected with family and friends who helped me through my fear of losing the game I loved.

I started hanging out with a long-time friend, Valerie, who had just broken up with her boyfriend.

We spent more and more time together. Soon we fell in love. Just when I thought I lost my career, I found something better.

Valerie held my hand through it all. We married two years later and now have two beautiful children. We wrote our own wedding vows. Mine said, "I give you my heart, and my right arm."

When I started throwing again it felt like learning the motion all over again.

I had no idea if I'd ever throw 80 mph. I talked to a lot of players who had the same surgery. They told me I could come back 100 percent if I worked hard. I believed them. I became dedicated to rebuilding my body and mind. I started reading books on psychology.

I MADE A SOLID COMEBACK IN 1998 PLAYING WITH THE VERO BEACH DODGERS IN FLORIDA. I POSTED A RESPECTABLE 9-7 RECORD.

The next season I moved up to the Class AA team in San Antonio. My arm felt great, but my eyesight started to blur. I noticed I couldn't focus on the signals from the catcher. I couldn't tell if the catcher was holding down one or more fingers.

Instead of dealing with the problem, I started guessing the signs. One night I guessed wrong and threw a curve when the catcher expected a fastball. It hit him in the chest. Before I killed our catcher, I got glasses.

The first game I wore glasses was a steamy night in Midland, Texas. The glasses fit too tightly on my face so when I started to heat up, they fogged. I had to stop between every single pitch and wipe my glasses. Talk about slowing down the game! Looser-fitting glasses solved that problem.

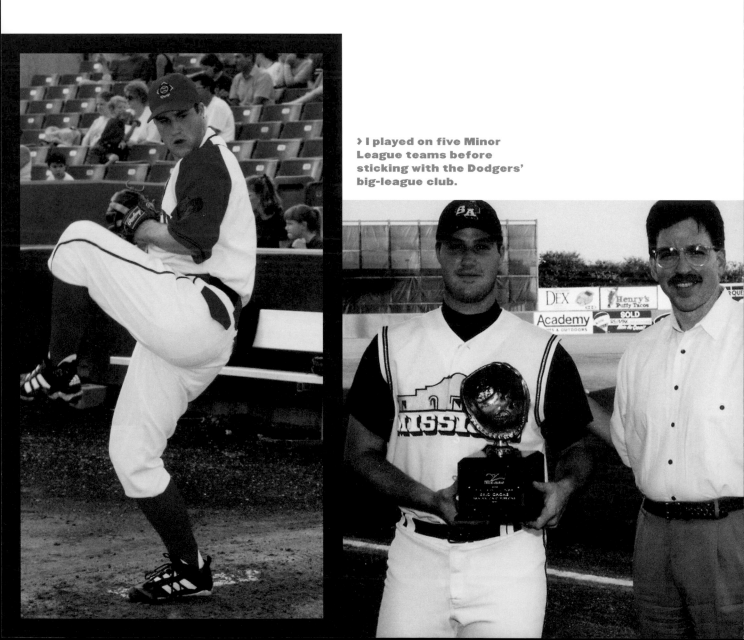

> I played on five Minor League teams before sticking with the Dodgers' big-league club.

THE SUMMER OF 1999 BECAME MY BREAKOUT SEASON. I WENT 12-4 WITH A LEAGUE-LEADING 185 STRIKEOUTS. I WAS NAMED TEXAS LEAGUE PITCHER OF THE YEAR AND THE DODGERS' BEST MINOR LEAGUE PITCHER.

MINOR LEAGUE **PITCHING** STATS

	W	L	SV	ERA	G	IP	H	R	ER	BB	KO	HR
South Atlantic League Savannah Sand Gnats	7	6	0	3.28	23	115.1	94	48	42	43	131	11
Florida State League Vero Beach Dodgers	9	7	0	3.74	25	139.2	118	69	58	48	144	16
Texas League San Antonio Missions	12	4	0	2.63	26	167.2	122	55	49	64	185	17
Pacific Coast League Albuquerque Dukes	5	1	0	3.88	9	55.2	56	30	24	15	59	8
Pacific Coast League Las Vegas 51s	3	0	0	1.52	4	23.2	15	4	4	8	31	2

My ultimate reward came with a call up to the Major Leagues in September. I pitched in five games. Before I called my parents to let them know the good news, I called Martin, the Montreal sportswriter. I told him I was going to pitch in the Major Leagues and thanked him for everything he wrote about me, including what I didn't want to hear.

My debut was special. It was against the Marlins in Florida. My family drove 24 hours straight to see me. Many friends showed up, including Dominic Campeau, my Canadian National teammate, who now is a high school coach in Florida.

Two problems popped up before my first pitch. I warmed up and couldn't throw a single strike in the bullpen. A terrible fear came over me that I was going to fail and lose under pressure.

Then rain delayed the game for three hours. That simmered my nervousness. My hands started shaking. Was this the Twilight Zone? I thought: "What is this? What's going on? I've never felt like this."

The time finally came to throw my first pitch. I calmed down once I got to the mound. I felt at home.

FIRST PITCH, STRIKE ONE. NEXT, STRIKE TWO. THEN STRIKE THREE. SECOND BATTER, STRIKEOUT. THIRD BATTER, GROUND OUT. I WENT SIX INNINGS AND STRUCK OUT EIGHT BATTERS FOR MY FIRST VICTORY.

I remember every pitch of that fabulous night. That experience showed me I could break barriers at the big-league level, starting with my own nerves, and win under pressure. I could channel my nervous energy into positive results.

FUN FACTS >>> ERIC'S FIRST MAJOR LEAGUE WIN CAME AGAINST FELLOW CANADIAN RYAN DEMPSTER. THEY WERE ROOMMATES ON THE CANADIAN NATIONAL TEAM. IT WAS THE FIRST TIME IN 25 YEARS TWO CANADIAN PITCHERS WENT HEAD TO HEAD IN THE MAJOR LEAGUES.

I slipped into mediocrity during the 2000 and 2001 seasons. I bounced up and down between the majors and minors seven times in two years. Valerie and I moved nine times in one year, and she was pregnant that year. My wife never complained once.

There have been times I've wanted to complain. Hearing disappointing news is never easy. The first time the Dodger staff said, "We've got to send you down," I had a positive comeback. I said, "I'll be back up. I know it."

Each demotion I promised myself I'd work harder. And I did.

I also called for an emotional reinforcement. I called home and asked Mom to send me my old, worn-out baby blanket. I just wanted it in my house. I keep it in a drawer.

Being a starter changed the way I pitched. I tried to pace myself. I nibbled on the corners rather than challenging hitters with more strikes. I wasn't being me. To break barriers sometimes you must be open to make changes.

I was ready for change. So in spring training of 2002 I talked with our coaches about being a reliever. I told them I'd do anything to stay on the team. Our closer from the previous year Jeff Shaw didn't return, so I got my chance.

A chance is all I needed. I always loved being a closer. Coming in with the game on the line, I could go all out for one or two innings and attack hitters.

Before I truly became a Major League closer, I needed a song. The stadium DJ asked me what I wanted as my introduction. I went with the first tune that popped into my head, "Welcome to the Jungle" by Guns N' Roses. When it's played the Dodger fans go wild and that motivates me.

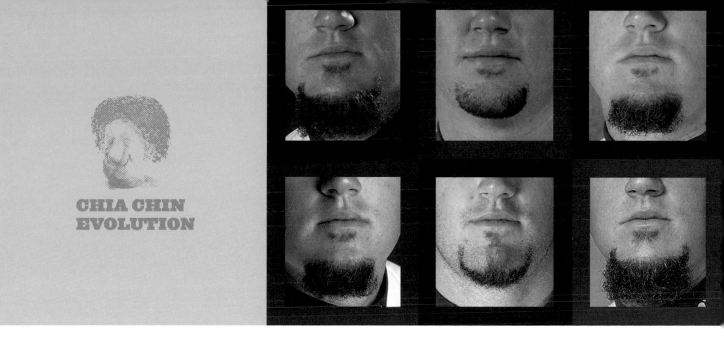

CHIA CHIN EVOLUTION

The song fits my personality, which is completely different off the field than on the field.

Off the field, I'm an easy-going guy. I'm a good listener (if I wasn't a baseball player I'd want to be a psychologist). I'm still a little shy speaking in public and meeting new people, although I'm improving.

I LIKE TO BE MY OWN PERSON, SO I'VE CHANGED MY LOOKS MANY TIMES OVER THE YEARS. I'VE BLEACHED MY HAIR BLOND. I'VE BEEN BALD. I'VE WORN A GOATEE (NICK-NAMED "CHIA CHIN"). I'VE HAD A PIERCED EYEBROW (UNTIL I HOOKED THE METAL BAR ON A PIECE OF CLOTHING AND IT RIPPED OUT). AND I HAVE TWO TATTOOS.

I have tattoos on both shoulders. One has a four-leaf clover with the initials ED, for Eric and Dave, my childhood friend. He has the same thing with the initials DE. The other shows a joker rolling dice. It's my reminder that you never know what's going to happen because you're always rolling the dice.

My wife says people ask her all the time if I'm mean to her at home. She'll tell you I'm a gentle giant—until I get onto the baseball diamond.

BUGS BUNNY CHANGE-UP

The purpose of a change-up is to fool the hitter and keep him off-balance.

A fastball is held almost as if you were giving the peace sign. There are many ways to grip a change-up. One is the "circle change." You throw it by making the "OK" sign with your hand—with pointer finger and thumb touching, thus creating a small circle. You then hold the ball in the three outside fingers. Throw this with the same arm action as a fastball and it will travel about 10 miles per hour slower than a fastball.

For the Bugs Bunny pitch, I hold the ball with a circle change grip and then split my middle two fingers apart. This makes the ball sink as well.

When I enter a home game with the outcome in doubt, the words "Game Over" are flashed on the big screen.

Becoming the Dodger closer changed my baseball career. I strung together save after save in 2002 and finished with 52, including eight in a row to end the season.

The streak continued in 2003 with a perfect closer record of 55-0 in save opportunities, which set a Major League record.

The streak and saves were great, but the numbers I'm most proud about that season were my strikeout-to-walk ratio. I booked 137 strikeouts with just 20 walks. Usually a 3-to-1 ratio is considered good. That means for every three strikeouts I walk one guy. That's my career ratio. Mine was more than twice as good in 2003 at almost 7:1. That means I'm throwing strikes and getting people out.

Besides my 97 mph fastball, I have a "Bugs Bunny" change-up and a curve-ball. I need all three pitches to be successful. I learned that off-speed pitch the year I hurt my arm. So if I hadn't been out a year, I probably wouldn't have married my wife and wouldn't have my second-best pitch. Events that seem unlucky at the time sometimes do turn out for the best. Likewise, when you fail, that experience will likely help you later on.

The Baseball Hall of Fame called me after the 2003 season. They requested my shoes and put my blue cleats alongside the greats of the game. I felt very honored. Winning the Cy Young Award was mind-blowing.

THE AWARD PUT ME FACE TO FACE WITH MY OLD FEAR OF SPEAKING TO AN AUDIENCE.

I'm cool with print and TV reporters before or after games. I've had lots of experience with that while playing baseball. On the day I won the Cy Young Award, I did live in-studio interviews at a couple Los Angeles TV stations during the day. Then I hit the late-night Jimmy Kimmel Live show. It turned out to be a fun experience.

CY YOUNG AWARD

Baseball Commissioner Ford Frick started an award for pitchers in 1956, noting pitchers rarely received attention in Most Valuable Player voting.

The award was named after pitcher Cy Young, who owns the Major League record for most career wins with 511; that's 95 more than Walter Johnson, No. 2 on the win list. Denton True "Cy" Young played on nine teams from 1890-1911. He died in 1955. Young won 30 games five times and won 20 games 15 times.

The award initially went to one pitcher deemed most valuable of both leagues. Don Newcombe won the first Cy Young Award with a 27-6 record for the Brooklyn Dodgers.

In 1974, Mike Marshall was the first reliever to win it. Furgeson Jenkins became the first Canadian to win a Cy Young Award in 1971.

> These are the shoes I wore when I earned my 55th consecutive save. They are now in the Baseball Hall of Fame.

That day I called many people—family, friends, and Coach Simmons. I thanked him for everything he did for me, and for turning my life around. I had written Coach Simmons a thank-you letter while in the minors but never sent it. I still have the letter. Coach said, "You did all the work. Don't stop now. Keep going. I'm so proud of you."

A few days after winning the Cy Young Award, I was back in Montreal. The city embraced me. I was invited to a Montreal Canadiens game to throw down the puck. The team gave me my own jersey with my name on it, and the fans gave me a standing ovation. The only thing that could've made it better was if I played in the hockey match.

When I play baseball, I become a different person. I'm a warrior. I want hitters to be intimidated by me.

I still get nervous before I pitch. But I'm not afraid.

My routine is to watch the first five innings of a game on TV in the club-house. Then I go to the bullpen. I get tense just sitting. I like to drink a Mountain Dew before I go in, but my hands will tremor some while holding the can.

WHEN I START WARMING UP, THAT'S WHEN I GET REVVED UP. I GO HYPER. I START TALKING IN FAST FORWARD. THE JITTERY BUTTERFLY FEELING TURNS INTO EXCITEMENT. I'M TOTALLY FOCUSED BY THE TIME I GET TO THE MOUND.

MAJOR LEAGUE **PITCHING** STATS

	Team	W	L	ERA	G	GS	CG	SHO	SV	SVO	IP	H	R	ER	HR	HBP	BB	SO
'99	LA	1	1	2.10	5	5	0	0	0	--	30.0	18	8	7	3	0	15	30
'00	LA	4	6	5.15	20	19	0	0	0	--	101.1	106	62	58	20	3	60	79
'01	LA	6	7	4.75	33	24	0	0	0	--	151.2	144	90	80	24	16	46	130
'02	LA	4	1	1.97	77	0	0	0	52	56	82.1	55	18	18	6	2	16	114
'03	LA	2	3	1.20	77	0	0	0	55	55	82.1	37	12	11	2	3	20	137

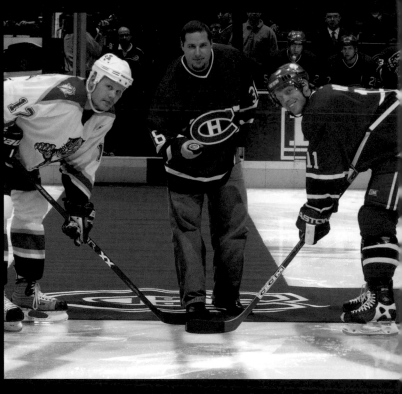

> I did blow one save in 2003—in the All-Star game. I laughed it off because hitters have the advantage. They know pitchers won't throw inside stuff in the showcase game.

> After winning the Cy Young Award, I returned to Montreal. My daughter and I giggle at seeing my dad and family at the Montreal airport. Later, I drop the puck before a Montreal Canadiens contest to fulfill a lifelong fantasy.

I forget about the pressure. Pressure is negative, and I don't build negative walls in my head.

If I said to myself before a pitch, "Oh no, what if this guy gets a hit and we lose? What if I blow the game? What will people say?"

I never think about the negative what-ifs. That's like putting garbage in your mouth. We all face enough real barriers in life. We don't have to add more with negative thinking. I visualize myself throwing a strike before each pitch. When I watch video of my performance, I never watch someone hitting a home run off me. I watch the strikeouts. I want to remember the strikeouts.

The other thing about the pressure barrier is perspective. There's life-and-death pressure and then there's everything else.

IF YOU FLUNK A TEST, LOSE A GAME, GO SPEECHLESS, OR LOSE A JOB, SO WHAT? YOU'LL HAVE OTHER CHANCES TO SUCCEED.

Now that I have a family of my own, if I have a bad baseball day and come home steaming mad, when I see the smiles of my children and wife I can't stay angry long. I smile, too. If I'm really stressing, I'll tiptoe into my daughter's room and just watch her sleep. It's the most beautiful thing in the world. It's so peaceful. That puts everything in perspective.

The way I see it, I can only control my thoughts and energies until the moment I release the ball. Then it's out of my hands. So before each pitch I tell myself how I'm going to get this batter out. I don't worry about what happens if he gets a hit or home run off me.

The way I break through is to allow myself to feel nervous. It's OK and natural to feel it. I just don't let it freak me out. Focus positively on what's in your hands and don't worry about what's out of your hands. Then do the best you can, roll the dice, and let life happen.

So when you are faced with stress and your heart is pounding, remember you can get through it. Like me, you can find ways to work through, over, or around your problems.

You too can break barriers.